EXPLORER BOOKS

JUNGLES & RAIN FORESTS

by
Julia L. Andrews

To
Louisa Margaret

Published by The Trumpet Club
1540 Broadway, New York, New York 10036

ISBN: 0-440-84533-5

Printed in the United States of America
November 1991

10 9 8 7 6 5 4 3 2
CW

PHOTOGRAPH CREDITS

p. 21: top, © Gregory G. Dimijian, M.D. 1986 / Photo Researchers, Inc.; *bottom,* © Robert W. Hernandez / Photo Researchers, Inc. *p. 22:* © 1989 Comstock, Inc. / Gwen Fidler. *p. 23: top,* © Tom McHugh / Photo Researchers, Inc.; *bottom,* © Francois Gohier / Photo Researchers, Inc. *p. 24: top,* © Gerry Ellis / The Wildlife Collection; *bottom,* © Alan Briere / Superstock. *p. 25: top,* © Animals Animals / Margot Conte; *bottom,* © 1988 Comstock, Inc. / Russ Kinne. *p. 26: top,* Earth Scenes / © Adrienne T. Gibson; *bottom,* Animals Animals / © Michael Fogden. *p. 27: top,* © 1990 Comstock, Inc. / Townsend P. Dickinson; *bottom,* © Ken Gibson / Superstock. *p. 28: top,* © Claudia Andujar / Photo Researchers, Inc.; *bottom,* © George Holton / Photo Researchers, Inc.

Cover: © Hubertus Kanus / Superstock.

Contents

Introduction

The rain forest has enchanted people for thousands of years. It's a magical, mysterious place filled with strange sounds, creatures, and gigantic plants. It's the only place on earth where you can find killer fish and 20-pound flowers! In fact, two-thirds of all the *species,* or kinds, of plants and animals on the planet live there. Did you know that people live in the rain forests, too? The rain forest is home to many of the world's ancient civilizations.

The first thing you'll notice in the rain forest is how green and wet everything looks. This is because the biggest rainstorm you can imagine drenches the forest almost every day. Trees as tall as skyscrapers shelter you from the hot tropical sun. Vines as thick as your waist wind their way through the trees. Animals that seem like fairy-tale creatures are everywhere. There's a monkey called a *pygmy marmoset* that's small enough to sit in a teacup. Another monkey, the *gibbon,* travels 30 feet in a single swing. You can also see butterflies with 12-inch wingspans.

In the rain forest looks can be deceiving. What looks like a twig on a tree may turn out to be a walking stick insect or a thin tree snake. Multicolored frogs whose skin may be orange with black polka dots or yellow with red squiggles can seem playful and harmless. But beware! Their skin oozes some of the world's deadliest poisons.

The rain forest may seem like a strange, faraway place that has nothing to do with you. Yet every day you eat, drink, or use something that comes from this part of the world. The rain forest gives us bananas, oranges, cinnamon, cocoa, and coffee. And how do you get to school—by bike or bus? Maybe you walk there in a pair of high tops. Tires and sneaker soles are made from rubber that grows in the rain forest. Bubble gum, too, is made with a substance that comes from this rubber. So you see, a day in the life of an average American boy or girl wouldn't be the same without the rain forest.

But something scary is happening. The rain forest is being destroyed by people. Each year an area of tropical forest the size of the state of Pennsylvania is ruined forever. By the time you're an adult, there may not be any rain forest left. Many things will change if this happens. Many plants and animals will become *extinct,* or cease to exist. There won't be as much clean air because there will be fewer plants. Like all plants, rain-forest trees produce a large amount of *oxygen*—the gas human beings and animals must breathe in order to live. If the trees are destroyed, there won't be as much oxygen.

Plants, animals, and oxygen are three reasons why people need rain forests. As you read this book, you'll discover many more reasons why we need to save the rain forests of the world. You'll also see just how amazing daily life in the rain forest is.

1

What Is a Rain Forest?

When It Rains, It Pours

The difference between a rain forest and other forests is rain, rain, and more rain. Rain forests get at least 70 inches of rain each year. *Temperate* forests, the kind that grow in the mild climates of North America and Europe, get only about half this amount each year.

Some rain forests get as much as 400 inches of rain each year. It would take 51 years for it to rain that much in Phoenix, Arizona. How much rain is 400 inches? To get an idea, put a jar outside the next time it rains and collect 1 inch of rain. The ground is pretty soggy after 1 inch of rain has fallen. Imagine 399 inches more. Now you know why these forests are called rain forests!

Because the rain forest is so wet, its trees have specially shaped leaves that work like raincoats. Although there are thousands of species of trees in the rain forest, they all have heart-shaped leaves with pointy tips. These *drip tips* allow the extra water to run off the leaves. Otherwise mold, which grows wherever it's damp, would turn the leaves into mush. Trees in temperate forests don't have this problem, so there aren't many drip-tip leaves there. There are, however, leaves in all shapes and colors—something you wouldn't see in the lush, green rain forest.

To see where most rain forests grow, run your hand over the widest part of a globe where the *equator* is located. The equator is the warmest place on earth. Rain forests grow mainly in the hot tropics near the equator in Africa, Asia, and Central and South America. There are also a few rain forests in North America. They can be found in Hawaii, on the Caribbean Islands, and even as far north as Washington State and Alaska.

What Is a Jungle?

You may think of rain forests as steaming hot jungles filled with roaring tigers. The truth is that most rain forests *are* steaming hot places and tigers *do* live there. But those forests aren't always *jungles*. Are rain forests and jungles the same thing? Yes and no. All jungles are rain forests, but not all rain forests are jungles. The word "jungle" comes from the word *jangala,* which means "thick vegetation" in *Sanskrit,* an ancient Indian language.

English travelers first explored India's rain forests in boats along the rivers. The only thing the explorers saw from their boats was a tangled mess of thick vines and huge plants growing along the riverbanks. They saw *jangala.* The explorers thought that the rest of the rain forest must be *jangala,* too. They never went deep inside the forest to see for themselves. Soon everyone was calling rain forests jungles.

But the travelers were wrong. Only part of the rain forest is actually jungle. Jungles, or patches of thick vegetation, crop up in any sunny area of the forest. That's why people find them along riverbanks and in clearings where a tree has fallen.

Even today, many people use the terms jungle and rain forest to mean the same thing. In this book, the word "jungle" is used to describe areas of overgrown plants in the rain forest. It doesn't mean the *whole* rain forest.

Layers of Life

When you first enter a rain forest, it looks like a tangled green mess. But it's really a very well-organized garden. Rain forests are divided into three distinct layers. Each layer has its own community of plants and animals. The top layer of the rain forest is called the *canopy*. It is formed by the thick, leafy tops of giant trees as tall as 15 flagpoles, or 300 feet. Monkeys, anteaters, birds, and most of the other animals in the forest live in the canopy.

Although many trees in the canopy tower 200 to 300 feet tall, their trunks are surprisingly skinny. Huge anchors, called *buttresses,* grow from the bottom of the trunks to hold the trees in place. These anchors are part of the trunk. They aren't separate plants. Buttresses look like giant fingers wrapped around the tree trunks.

Just beneath the treetops in the canopy is a layer made up of shorter trees and their branches. This layer is called the *understory*. A different group of creatures roam around the understory. Wild cats called *ocelots* prowl for prey. Bats, tree frogs, and vipers (a kind of poisonous snake) lurk in the leaves. Birds and butterflies flutter everywhere.

The bottom layer, the *forest floor,* is covered with tiny shrubs and young plants. It's dark, hot, and damp here, and the air barely moves. The forest floor is covered with billions of ants and other insects. There are also wild pigs, deer, and huge hairy spiders called *tarantulas.* In the movies, people exploring the rain forest always seem to need razor-sharp machetes to hack their way through a sea of monstrous vines. In real life, though, the forest floor is actually clear and tidy.

Although the tropical sun beats down on most rain forests 12 hours a day, the inside of the forest is a dark, shadowy place. The canopy blocks out most of the light. Only 1/100 of the day's sunshine ever reaches the forest floor. This makes life very difficult for the plants there! They need sun and water in order to grow. There's certainly plenty of water in the rain forest, but there isn't much sun. To survive, the plants go into a resting stage, waiting for a tree to fall and open up a hole in the canopy. When this happens, the plants can finally get the sun they need. But the wait for sunshine can take years. That's why the forest floor seems so clear—not much grows there.

The Greatest Show on Earth

Rain forests have been around for 200 million years. They're older than any other lifeform on Earth. Some of the first creatures to live in the rain forest were the dinosaurs. At that time, rain forests covered most of the land. Even Antarctica, which is frozen tundra today, was once a warm and humid rain forest. Over millions of years, the forests have changed quite a bit. Today they are filled with flowers, bats, birds, butterflies, and billions of insects that didn't exist during the age of the dinosaurs.

The world's largest and most famous rain forest stretches for 3 million square miles across South America in the region where the Amazon River flows. The entire continental United States could fit inside this forest. Called *Amazonia,* this region is home to more living things than are found anywhere else in the world. More than 20 million species of insects alone live in Amazonia. One scientist counted 43 different species of ants living in a single tree in Peru. That's how many species there are in the huge country of Canada.

Life in the rain forest never stops changing. For example, a plant might develop a poison in its leaves to prevent animals from eating it. Or an animal's color might change so that it blends into the background and can hide from enemies. Using color to hide is called *camouflage.* These changes take place very slowly during many generations. Being able to change, or *adapt,* is the key to survival for all plants and animals. This is what has allowed the rain forest to survive on earth for millions of years.

2

Life at the Top

In the forests of North America, life in the treetops is mainly for the birds. But in the rain forest, you don't need wings to spend your life at the top. Snakes, frogs, lizards, and mammals of all shapes and sizes live up high with the bugs and birds. *Mammals* are warm-blooded animals that produce milk to feed their young. You are a mammal, and so are cats and dogs. All of these animals may wander down to the lower branches in the forest understory, or even to the ground in search of food. However, their home is mainly high in the treetops.

Why Sloths Are Slugs

One of the most curious creatures in the rain forest is the sloth. The word *sloth* means "laziness." Anybody who has ever seen this animal can tell you how it got its name: It's the slowest mammal on earth. When a sloth moves (which isn't very often), it looks as if it's moving in slow motion. It travels about 6 feet a minute. At that speed, it would take 15 hours to travel 1 mile. (It takes you only 20 minutes to walk 1 mile.) When a sloth moves at top speed, it goes about 14 feet a minute.

Sloths are the size of large, fat cats. They're 2 feet long, weigh about 12 pounds, and live in the rain forests of Central and South America. There are 2-toed and 3-toed sloths. (A sloth's toe works like a claw.) The sloths we see today evolved from the giant sloth that lived thousands of years ago during the Ice Age. At that time, a sloth was as big as an elephant!

The sloth is helpless on the ground. It can't run or walk! All it can do is drag its body around, which makes it easy prey for hungry jaguars.

A sloth in a tree, however, is another story. The sloth spends its life upside down, hanging from the branches of the tall *Cecropia* tree. The sloth eats, sleeps, mates, and even gives birth upside down. For meals, it plucks leaves and twigs from the tree. The sloth doesn't drink water because it gets all the liquid it needs from leaves. It doesn't fall because it has sharp, 3-inch-long toes on its four feet. By digging its clawed toes into a branch, a sloth can hang in one spot for days. Even dead sloths cling to branches. People don't hunt them because they're too hard to pry away from trees.

Once in a while, however, a sloth does topple out of a tree. With luck, it falls into a river and not onto the ground. Although it's a terrible walker, the sloth is a good, fast swimmer. It swims easily on its back and can also do a stroke that looks like the crawl.

Sloths are also champion sleepers. They spend up to 18 hours sleeping, barely moving the entire time. Staying still is an excellent defense against enemies. The sloth's stillness makes it look like dried leaves hanging from a branch. This is a form of camouflage. To complete the picture, green algae grows on the sloth's grayish-brown fur. This allows the animal to blend in perfectly with the trees.

The Perfect Picnic Guest

Ants are everywhere in the rain forest, from the treetops to the forest floor. And wherever there are ants, you'll find mammals called *anteaters.* If you invited an anteater to a picnic, you wouldn't have to worry about sharing your bologna sandwich with an army of ants. The anteater would eat all the ants!

Even when they're hundreds of feet off the ground, anteaters crawl expertly from branch to branch in search of the perfect meal: a mouthful of ants or termites. An anteater eats about 35,000 ants every day. It doesn't have teeth, and its mouth is no wider than a pencil. How, then, does it manage to eat such huge meals?

An anteater has a 22-inch-long tongue that's covered with very sticky saliva. The animal begins by sniffing out an anthill or termite mound and using its powerful claws to dig a little hole in it. It then whips its tongue in and out of the hole as quickly as 160 times a minute. The poor ants don't stand a chance. Anteaters move their tongues so quickly to avoid being stung by the ants or termites. (They're smart enough to steer clear of ants with the most poisonous stings, such as *army ants* and *giant black ants.*)

Even though anteaters devour thousands of ants a day, they never eat too many from one colony. If they did, the colony would be destroyed and they would run out of food. An anteater spends about a minute slurping a few hundred ants from one nest, then it moves on to another colony. One scientist watched an anteater stop at 49 anthills within a single hour.

A close relative of the sloth, the anteater lives in the rain forests and grasslands of Latin America. The *silky anteater,* which is the size of a squirrel, lives up in the trees and hunts for termite colonies nestled in the branches. The *giant anteater* is 7 feet long. It spends its days sniffing out meals on the ground. Although anteaters look mild-mannered, they're fierce fighters. If another animal threatens them, they lash out with razor-sharp claws. Even deadly jaguars and mountain lions avoid these claws.

The Tiny Terror

The *Dayak* tribe lives in the rain forests of North Borneo in Indonesia. They are very brave hunters. But there is one animal that makes them tremble with fear—the *tarsier.* If you've ever seen a tarsier, you'll probably wonder why the Dayaks are so afraid of it. This tiny creature is the size of a chipmunk and weighs the same as 4 slices of bread— about 4 ounces. Tarsiers and monkeys are close relatives. Tarsiers, monkeys, gorillas, apes, and humans are all members of a large group of animals called *primates.* Primates use their fingers to grasp objects.

Tarsiers are found in the thick jungles of Indonesia and the Philippines. They are *nocturnal,* which means that they sleep during the day and become active at night. They feed on insects, frogs, and lizards. The tarsier's enormous, bulging eyes are its most unusual feature. They take up one-third of the animal's skull. If a tarsier's head were as big as yours, its eyes would be as big as apples! The tarsier's eyes are its best hunting tools.

Like owls, bats, and other nocturnal creatures, tarsiers need to be able to spot their prey in the dark. Large eyes work much better at night than do small ones. With eyes like these, tarsiers have no trouble making out shapes in the dark.

Even with their huge eyes, tarsiers don't seem very frightening. Why are the Dayak so terrified of them? Tarsiers are always on the lookout for food and foes. Like a windup toy that won't stop moving, the animal constantly spins its head this way and that to see what—or who—is around. In fact, it can swivel its head around 180 degrees to face backwards. Dayak hunters believe that if a tarsier twists its head around backward to stare at a warrior, that warrior will lose his head in battle.

Monkey Business

A *zoologist,* a scientist who studies the behavior of animals, named Michael Robinson first arrived in a small village in Panama to study tropical insects during the 1960's. People warned him, "Watch out for jaguars! Listen for their roar!" One day he was alone in the jungle when a thunderous roar boomed through the air. Although he was terrified, he wanted to see the magnificent cat. But it wasn't a jaguar. It was a howler monkey! (Actually, jaguars don't roar; they just grunt loudly.)

Howler monkeys are the largest monkeys in the New World (the area that includes North, Central, and South America). They inhabit rain forests from southern Mexico all the way down to Argentina. Howler monkeys have huge roars that can be heard 3 miles away. They roar, or howl, for the same reasons wolves howl, sending out a message loud and clear—"No trespassing! This is our turf."

Howler monkeys have *prehensile* tails, as do all monkeys from the New World. Prehensile tails are adapted for seizing or holding objects. In fact, you can tell what part of the world a monkey is from by examining its tail. If it has a prehensile tail, it lives in the New World. If it has an ordinary tail, it lives in the Old World, which includes the continents of Europe, Africa, and Asia. A prehensile tail works like an extra hand or foot. A monkey uses its tail to balance itself in the trees, to grab food, and to hold objects. Sometimes a monkey uses its tail instead of its feet to move. In addition, monkeys have "tail prints" on the underside of their tails. These are like the fingerprints people have. These prints help both people and monkeys to get a better grip on things.

Because monkeys have so many limbs for gripping things (two feet, two hands, a tail), they rarely fall out of trees. One day, however, a zoologist named Kenneth Glander was observing a *troop,* or family of monkeys, in Costa Rica's rain forest. As he watched, a female howler high up in the trees seemed to get dizzy. She fell to the ground, 35 feet below. She wasn't badly hurt, and she soon climbed back up to the branches. Earlier, Glander had found the dead bodies of several howler monkeys on the ground. Why did these monkeys fall and die? Was a mysterious disease killing the troop?

After much scientific detective work, Glander discovered the cause of death. There was poison in the monkeys' food. The tender leaves of the *madera negra* trees that the monkeys had feasted on were loaded with *rotenone,* a poison used to kill rats. Like many plants, these trees produce poison to prevent themselves from being eaten. The number of dead howler monkeys lying beside the tree trunks was proof that the poison worked. The female that Glander saw was lucky. She hadn't eaten enough of the poison to kill her.

Some animals eat *toxic,* or poisonous, plants without having any problems at all. A relative of the monkeys, the *golden bamboo lemur,* eats pounds of toxic plants every day. The lemur lives in Madagascar, a country that has some of the world's most spectacular rain forests. The animal gets its name from its favorite food, the golden bamboo. This plant is loaded with *cyanide,* a very dangerous chemical that can kill humans. Yet the lemur eats the golden bamboo every day and never gets sick. However, if the golden bamboo lemur ate leaves from the *madera negra* trees, it would probably end up like the howler monkeys—poisoned to death.

Talking Birds

Parrots thrive in hot, humid weather. Wherever you find rain forests, you'll find parrots. (They've lived there for millions of years.) In fact, one-third of all the birds in the world nest there. Almost all of these birds live at the very top of the forest canopy.

Parrot feathers come in every spectacular color you can imagine. They're an important part of the birds' body language. A male shows off his long, colorful tail to a possible mate. If the female likes what she sees, she accepts him. A male parrot chases other males away from his mate by ruffling the red feathers on its shoulders. Though adult parrots are colorful creatures, newborn parrots look like lumps of pink clay. They don't grow beautiful feathers until they're a few months old.

As many bird owners know, parrots can imitate all kinds of words and strange sounds. But do the birds understand what they're saying? Some scientists believe they do. Dr. Irene Pepperberg, a scientist in Illinois, has been studying how birds talk and think for more than 12 years. The star of her project is Alex, an African gray parrot. Alex knows hundreds of words, can identify the shapes and colors of objects, and carries on conversations with humans. After talking with Alex for 12 years, Dr. Pepperberg has come to believe that parrots think before they squawk.

Parrots are small but mighty birds. A tiny parrot can apply 300 pounds of pressure with a strong squeeze of its beak. It's nimble enough to peel a tender grape and strong enough to crunch through a thick piece of wood. Parrots feed on Brazil nuts and other tropical plants that are covered with very tough protective shells, or rinds. A parrot's beak makes an excellent nutcracker.

Parrots are great climbers, too. Unlike most birds, their feet are built for grabbing and climbing up trees. They also use their feet to pick up food. Parrots, like humans, use one limb more than the other. Most parrots are left-footed.

Faster Than a Speeding Bullet

Everything about a hummingbird is fast! By the time you count to 60, a hummingbird will have beat its wings 4,500 times. The wings whip back and forth so rapidly that they hum. This movement is too fast for the human eye to see. The bird's heart beats

1,260 times a minute. It flies as fast as a speeding car—71 miles per hour.

Hummingbirds, sometimes called hummers, are found only in the New World. Because these birds are so small, people sometimes mistake them for insects. The minuscule *bee hummingbird* is the size of a dime! No bigger than a bee! It's the world's tiniest bird.

We have hummingbirds to thank for many of the spectacular flowers found in tropical climates. The birds help *fertilize* the flowers by spreading pollen from one plant to another. Over thousands of years, the shapes of the flowers and the birds' bodies have changed so that they fit together like the pieces of a puzzle. This makes it much easier for the bird to get food, and for the flower to spread its pollen. When two living things change, or *evolve,* together, it is called *coevolution.*

The rain forest is filled with giant ferns, thick vines, and 300-foot-tall trees.

An Asmat warrior of New Guinea holds a figure of an ancestor.

This unfortunate green lynx spider is about to become a meal
for a pitcher plant.

The huge eyes of this Philippine tarsier take up ⅓ of its skull. They enable the tarsier to hunt at night.

The 3-toed sloth digs its clawed toes into a branch. It can hang upside down in one spot for days.

The jaguar is the biggest wildcat in the New World. It is about 6 feet long and weighs up to 250 pounds.

The ocelot is another wildcat that prowls the understory of the rain forest searching for prey.

The white-handed gibbon, a type of monkey, travels 30 feet in a single swing.

The white-lipped peccary, or wild pig, is hunted by some rain-forest people for food.

The rafflesia flower is nicknamed "the corpse lily" because it smells like a dead body. A single bloom measures 3 feet across and weighs 20 pounds!

This Peruvian anteater catches about 35,000 ants a day with its 22-inch-long tongue.

Army ants got their name because they march in well-organized columns. They devour every insect, reptile, and bird in their path.

Iguanas live high up in the canopy of the rain forest. Panamanians are learning how to raise them for food.

The Yanomami Indians of Brazil practice the same customs that were a way of life for their ancestors.

These two Lacondan Maya girls live in the rain forest of southern Mexico. There are only about 250 of these Indians left.

3

Tropical Terrors

Every inch of the rain forest is filled with animals. Are all these exotic creatures dangerous? The truth is that there are only a few real live monsters in the rain forest. Some of these tropical terrors are the stars of Hollywood's creepiest creature features. Read about the insects, snakes, big cats, bats, and killer fish that live in the rain forest, so you can see whether the terrible things you've heard about them are true!

Ants in Your Plants

Streams of *army ants* crawling in every direction are a common sight in the rain forest. They're always on the lookout for food. Anything small or slow enough to be wrestled by the ants turns into supper. They prey on other insects, spiders, centipedes, lizards, snakes, and baby birds. Army ants live in Africa, South America, and Central America. Some have even made it as far north as New Jersey!

Like human soldiers, army ants march in well-organized columns. These columns are about 1 foot wide and as long as a football field. Some stretch on for an entire mile! Many times the columns split up and the ants begin moving in many different directions. The ants have just received a command or message. Ants communicate by releasing chemicals called *pheromones*. Each pheromone has a distinct odor that sends a certain message. The ants release one kind of pheromone when there's food nearby, for example, and another when an enemy is close. They pick up the messages with their antennae. When ant leaders find prey, they pierce the victim with their powerful jaws and inject it with a poisonous substance called *venom*. As they deliver the bite, they release the "dinner" pheromone. Within seconds, millions of other ants rush in to devour the kill.

Army ants won't attack humans—unless you step into a column, that is. Then, of course, the insects will race up your legs and try to bite you. The stings hurt, but they won't kill you.

There is, however, one ant in the rain forest you should definitely avoid. The *bullet ant* delivers a nasty bite that stings for a long time. The ant itself makes tiny screams as it stings. Stumble into a nest of these noisy monsters, and hundreds of them will stab their sharp stingers into your leg. One of these bites could make you very ill. Hundreds of these bites could make a person go into shock—and even die!

Miniature Monsters

When people visit a rain forest, they usually worry about being killed by poisonous snakes or ferocious jaguars. The chances of this happening are slim. The real dangers in the forest are tiny, harmless-looking animals.

One of these little monsters is the *botfly*. When these flies first hatch, they look like tiny white worms. At this stage flies are called *maggots*. Botfly maggots feed on warm, living mammal flesh. Often that flesh belongs to a person. The maggots dig beneath the person's skin and live there for weeks, eating flesh the entire time. As the maggots grow, they create a lump as big as an egg in their victim's skin. You can even see them squirming around. Once in a while, the botflies dig deep under the skin and form a bump on a vital organ such as the liver or kidney. This can be extremely dangerous because the insects could slowly poison their victim.

Sometimes the maggots go away on their own. (One man who had had a bump on his head for many weeks was at a Boston Red Sox baseball game when he felt the maggots slither out of his skin.) If they don't, it may not be easy to get rid of these pests. Surgery doesn't always work—some of the maggots stay in the skin. However, one cure that's used in the tropics seems to work very well. Raw meat is wrapped tightly over the bump. It could take weeks, but eventually the maggots leave the skin and dig a new home in the meat. Then the meat and the maggots are thrown away.

Big, Bad, and Boa

Deep in the jungles of the West Indies and South America live the innocent victims of tall tales and rumors. These victims are the *boas,* the world's largest snakes. People accuse these slinky giants of being mean, man-eating machines. But boas are *not* ferocious. They're not even poisonous! They'd rather flee than fight. Like most animals, however, they protect themselves when they are in danger.

Boas are the longest animals on land. Two of the most famous members of the group are the *boa constrictor* and the *anaconda.* The longest boa constrictor measured 18½ feet long—that's about 3 times longer than a tall man. However, the constrictor is short compared with the anaconda. The anaconda, the world's longest snake, is longer than a school bus. From head to tail, it is almost 40 feet long. The record for the world's heaviest snake also goes to the anaconda. One weighed 600 pounds—as much as 10 fourth-graders!

Anacondas live in jungle swamps and streams. Like all boas, they are slow movers. Anacondas don't chase their prey. Instead, they wait for their prey to come to them. They feed on birds and small mammals such as deer and *peccaries,* or wild pigs. When these unlucky animals wander by the water's edge, the anaconda makes its move. First the snake drags its victim into the water. Then it coils its body around the animal and squeezes. It squeezes so hard that the animal can't breathe and dies of suffocation. Death by *constriction,* or squeezing, is the way all boas kill their prey.

Boas aren't messy killers. They don't turn their victims into a bloody pulp, and they rarely break any bones. They simply swallow the animal whole as soon as it stops breathing. Like most snakes, boas have special jaws that allow them to swallow animals that are much wider than they themselves are. Boas aren't wasteful either. Super strong digestive juices turn the victim's entire body into useful nutrition. One boa that ate a porcupine digested everything, even the quills! After a big meal of porcupine or pig, it's usually several weeks before the snake feels the urge to eat again.

Boa constrictors don't eat people. They can't swallow an animal as large as a human! Neither can most anacondas, even though their name means "elephant killer." There's only one case in which an anaconda may actually have swallowed someone. A 13-year-old boy vanished while swimming in a river. His friend saw an anaconda nearby. When the boy's body was found, it looked as though the snake had vomited it up.

King of the Cats

To prove their manhood and become warriors, young Indian men in the forests of Bolivia must kill a jaguar. A wooden spear is the only weapon they are allowed to use. This is an extremely dangerous ritual. The man who fails may pay with his life.

The jaguar is king of the rain forest. Its name means "he who kills in one leap." This big cat is a swift and brutal killer. When hunting, it hides up in the branches of the trees, waiting for a peccary or some other mammal to pass below. Then, silently, the jaguar pounces onto the back of its victim. It digs powerful claws deep into the animal's flesh to hold it in place for the next deadly move. Lions and tigers rip their victims' throats apart. When the jaguar attacks, however, it wraps its massive jaws around the animal's skull and cracks it open, killing the animal instantly.

The biggest cat in the New World, the jaguar is about 6 feet long and weighs between 100 and 250 pounds. You'd think it would be hard to miss such a large creature, yet jaguars are almost impossible to see in the wild. The black and tan spots on their fur provide excellent camouflage. Jaguars are nocturnal animals, like tarsiers. With their great padded paws, they move silently through the forest understory, hidden by the night's darkness. After an evening of prowling and pouncing, a jaguar spends the day lounging in a tree.

The ancient *Maya,* a group of people who once lived in Latin America, believed that the jaguar's spots represented stars in the sky. To them, the jaguar was the god of the night, the ruler of the underworld. They thought it was the jaguar that had given humans the gift of fire. For centuries, many tribes have worshiped this sleek, powerful animal.

The jaguar may be mighty in the animal kingdom, but it is powerless against humans armed with guns. So many jaguars have been killed that the animal is now an *endangered* species. It is in danger of becoming extinct. Although there are laws against killing jaguars, poachers ignore them and continue to shoot the animals for their beautiful fur. At one time jaguars could be found anywhere from the middle of South America to the southern United States. American ranchers worried that the jaguars would kill their cattle, so they shot all the big cats. Now the jaguar is extinct in the United States, and no one knows how many are living in South America. Today the only truly safe place for a jaguar is the zoo.

Friendly Vampires

At night in the rain forest you may hear the "whoosh" of a *vampire bat*'s flapping wings as it scans the ground below for the perfect victim. Then it spots its prey sleeping beside a tree. Quietly and quickly, the bat moves in to make a tiny slash in its victim's skin and laps up the oozing blood. It stops drinking only when its stomach is full. This vampire bat drank the blood of a *tapir,* a large South American mammal that looks like a furry hog.

Bats are the only mammals that fly. There are 1,000 species of them in the world, but only three of these species are bloodsuckers. The other 997 species feed on fruits, flowers, fish, frogs, birds, or insects. (Each bat species eats only one kind of food.) The largest bat is a fruit-eater from Australia and Africa. From wing tip to wing tip, this bat is 6 feet wide! The tiny *hog-nose bat,* found in the rain forests of Thailand, is the world's smallest mammal. It's as light as a penny.

Vampire bats are found only in the tropics of Central and South America. Like all bats, the vampire bat is nocturnal. It hates bright light and will fly to a dark spot if it is placed in the sun. Vampire bats live inside protected caves in large groups called *roosts*. The only time they leave the cave is for 2 hours every night when they thirst for blood. Vampire bats feed on mammals such as tapirs, peccaries, and cows. (They rarely bite humans. When they do, however, they drink only a tablespoon or two of blood.)

Unlike most bats, which catch their prey in mid-air, vampire bats locate their prey, land on the ground, then climb on top of their victims. Only then do they bite. Other bats are very clumsy on land, but vampires have pads on their wings that help them to hop and climb easily.

Once a vampire bat finds blood, it drinks for about 10 minutes. Vampire bats drink $1\frac{1}{3}$ times their body weight in blood each night. That sounds like a lot of blood, but it isn't. The bat weighs only $1\frac{1}{2}$ ounces—as much as a large cookie.

Believe it or not, vampire bats aren't ferocious animals. Like all bats, they're shy, caring creatures. If one vampire bat is sick and can't hunt, other bats will spit up blood and share their food.

Killer Fish

If you're on one of the many rivers that wind through the rain forests of Latin America, and you'd like to see a piranha, pour a tiny drop of blood into the water. Hundreds of them will rush to the spot in search of a fresh meal. *Piranhas* are small, ferocious fish that are usually about 8 inches long. Some species grow as long as 2 feet, however.

Of all the deadly animals in the rain forest, the *carnivorous,* or meat-eating, piranha is the most vicious. Several thousand of them hunt together in huge groups called *schools.* They swarm together in such large numbers that the rivers look as if they're filled with fish instead of water. A school of piranhas can turn a big, fat cow into a skeleton in less than a minute. The fish scrape every ounce of skin and meat from the bones of their prey. This makes them very tidy butchers. Instead of ripping the meat off their victims, piranhas neatly slice it off. Their teeth are extremely pointy and are as sharp as razors. They have some of the sharpest teeth in the animal kingdom!

Piranhas are so aggressive that they'll even attack one another. Villagers who live near piranha-infested rivers know how aggressive these little fish can be. In some of these villages, many people have lost toes or fingers by dangling a foot or hand in a river that was filled with piranhas. These fish usually live off other, smaller fish. But they'll attack any living thing that floats their way. People in Brazil tell the story of a man on horseback who rode into a river that was filled with piranhas. The fish ate all the flesh off the man and his horse within a few minutes. However, they didn't touch the man's clothes!

4

People of the Forest

Animals aren't the only mammals that live in the rain forest. Today about 200 million people live in rain forests around the world. Most of them live deep inside the forest, far away from modern cities and highways. To reach their homes, you'd have to paddle up a river or hike through the forest for several days. Many of these people are descendants of ancient tribes. Their lifestyle seems simple to city dwellers. However, it is a way of life that has helped these tribes survive for thousands of years.

Michu Grows Up

Michu Valanzuela is a Mayan Indian boy who lives in the rain forest in southeastern

Mexico. Although his home is less than 1,000 miles away from Mexico City, his life is very different from that of a city boy. Michu doesn't go to school, watch television, or play video games. There is no refrigerator in his house. Like everyone else in his tiny village, Michu lives with his family in a hut made of palm leaves and vines. He spends his days hunting wild pigs or fishing with his father. He helps his mother pick fruits and grow corn, the family's main food. Sometimes Michu paddles around a nearby lake in the canoe that his grandfather carved from a huge mahogany tree. To cool down from the forest heat, he dives into the lake. But first, he checks the water for crocodiles.

Michu's tribe, the *Lacondan Maya,* has lived in this forest for thousands of years. Michu will grow up in the same way that his ancestors did thousands of years ago. He will learn the same things they learned in order to survive in the rain forest.

Halfway around the world, in the rain forest of western Africa, three brothers learn similar lessons for survival. These boys are members of the *Lese* tribe. Like Michu, they live in a hut and don't go to school the way you do. The rain forest is their school.

The Lacondan Maya of Latin America and the Lese of Africa are just two of the tribes that live in rain forests around the world. Not all rain forest people are alike. Each tribe has its own language, myths, and customs. Some tribes build villages and settle in one spot for several years. Others travel around the forest hunting for animals. Some fear any contact with people from the modern world. Others like modern conveniences and welcome changes in their life-style. Despite these differences, the tribes share an important belief: They respect the rain forest and have learned to *conserve,* or protect, its resources. They know that if they abuse the forest, they will destroy their homeland.

Growing up in the rain forest isn't easy. In many rain forests, only half of all babies born live past their second birthday. Adults often die by the time they are 40 or 45 years old. Sometimes food is very scarce. Finding clean water is another problem. The ponds from which the villagers get their drinking water may be filled with insects that carry deadly diseases.

Entire tribes of Indians living in the Latin American rain forests have been killed by two diseases that many Americans get without becoming seriously ill—measles and the flu. The Indians aren't *immune* to these diseases. In other words, their bodies aren't able to fight off the germs that cause these illnesses. As a result, they die. Infected outsiders expose the Indians to the germs when they visit their villages.

The Shortest People

The *Mbuti* (um-BOO-tee) *Pygmies* of West Africa believe that the rain forest is a parent that provides them with food, shelter, and protection. When someone dies or hunting is bad, the Pygmies believe that the rain forest is asleep and has forgotten to guard its children. The tribe sings and dances to wake up the forest. They hope the festival will please the forest so that it will be kind to them again.

Pygmies have lived in the rain forests for many thousands of years. During this time, their bodies have evolved in such a way that they have become small and lightweight. Pygmies are the shortest people in the world. A full-grown Pygmy man is only 4 1/2 feet—about as tall as an average American 10-year-old. This size is a big advantage in the rain forest. It allows the Pygmies to climb trees very quickly to capture animals and find hives of honey, which is a favorite treat. But getting this treat is hard work. The men must climb up tall trees and tear open beehives. Naturally, the bees don't like this very much, and they sting the thieves. The men put up with the pain and gather the honey anyway.

Pygmies are very peaceful, friendly people. They arrange their huts so that the doorways face the hut of a good friend. If one Pygmy is upset with another, he may turn his doorway away from that person. If someone has committed a crime, everyone turns their doorways away from that person. To keep the criminal out of sight, the tribe puts up wooden screens called *spite fences*. But the punishment doesn't last long. Soon the screens are taken down, and the criminal is welcomed back into the tribe.

Pygmies live in groups of 20 to 100 people. The group moves around the forest from one season to another in search of good hunting grounds. Hunting is a big social event in which everyone participates. Some groups hunt with arrows that have been dipped into poison. Whoever shoots the arrow that kills the game has first choice of the best meat.

Other Pygmies hunt with enormous nets. These nets are prized possessions that are handed down from father to son. Made from vines, they are as wide as a tennis net and as long as an Olympic swimming pool. The men string several nets across the forest. Women and children chase game out of the bushes by making a lot of noise. Even pet dogs get into the act!

Once antelope or other game become entangled in the nets, the men stab them with poison-tipped spears. After a successful hunt for animals or honey, the men celebrate by folding their arms and patting themselves. This is their way of thanking the forest for the gift of food.

Fighting for Survival

A few rain-forest tribes have steered clear of the modern world in order to hold on to their ancient way of life. The *Tasady* tribe of the Philippines wasn't discovered by Europeans until 1971. These people live just as they did thousands of years ago. Everyone lives in one big cave. Their food is made up of nuts, fruits, and fish. They speak their own language, which has no word for "war." They do not understand this kind of violence, so they have no weapons. Today there are only about 24 Tasadys left. Although they have survived for thousands of years, they are now in danger of dying out. Timber companies are building roads and destroying the forests where the tribe lives. Soon the Tasadys will have nowhere to go.

The *Penan* tribe lives on the island of Borneo in Indonesia. The people of this tribe face the very same problems that threaten the Tasadys. Logging companies want to cut down timber in the Penan's territory. This will not only destroy the tribe's home, it will anger their gods. The Penan refuse to cut down any trees because they believe there are powerful forest spirits. In 1987, when the loggers tried to move in, the Penan fought back. They hid in the forests, armed with poison arrows and blowpipes. Loggers who chopped down trees were killed. The government closed down the roads to the area. For now, at least, logging has stopped.

Brain-Eating Cannibals

Kuru is the rarest disease in the world. It gives people terrible seizures and eventually kills them. There's only one way to catch kuru—by eating human brains! Occasionally members of the *Asmat* tribe in Papua, New Guinea, die of kuru. They are *cannibals*—they eat human beings.

Asmats don't eat people because they're hungry. It is a spiritual act. Many tribes in the jungle islands of the South Pacific used to practice this ritual. Cannibal tribes, including the Asmats, are fierce hunters who once waged wars with other tribes to settle disputes. After a bloody battle, Asmat tribesmen ate their victims' bodies to honor the victims' strength and courage. They didn't eat the entire body, however, just the brain and the thigh. A warrior would then cut off a victim's head and wear it around his waist to show his bravery. Also, it was believed that if the warrior kept a victim's head close to his body, the victim's spirit couldn't seek revenge. Many Asmat villages had a head house where everyone displayed the severed heads of their enemies. The head house was the center of village life. With rows of dried heads staring from the walls, the village men would hold

46

council meetings, make tribal decisions, and plan battles. Until recently, cannibalism was a very popular form of warfare among the Asmats. The practice is now dying out, however.

Ancient Ways in the Amazon

When Spanish explorers returned from the Amazon during the 1500's, they told tales about natives with dogs' heads, one-legged flying men, and tribes of bat people. The tales were false, but they scared the strangers away. The Indians were glad that the explorers were afraid to return. Outsiders weren't welcome. The Indians enjoyed the lifestyle they had in their rain-forest homes.

The *Yanomami* Indians are the largest group of forest dwellers in Amazonia who still have a traditional lifestyle. They practice the same customs that were a way of life for their ancestors. Because they live in the thick forests of Brazil and Venezuela, they have not yet been affected by modern civilization. As a result, their lifestyle has remained the same for generations.

The Yanomamis live together in a large palm hut. For food, they hunt and grow crops on small plots of land. Clearing land in the rain forest is no easy task. The Indians set fire to the trees, then clear the debris before they begin farming. This method, used by tribes around the world for thousands of years, is called *slash-and-burn.* Because the soil is so poor, crops grow in one plot for only a few years. When the soil gives out, the tribe moves to a new area to start over again. The Yanomamis once waged war against other Yanomami villages. Now they have a new enemy.

The government has declared that the Indians' territory is a *preserve,* or protected area. But the Brazilian army plans to build a road along its border with Venezuela in order to patrol the region. The price of this road is the destruction of huge chunks of the Yanomamis' homeland. Gold miners and others also constantly invade the preserve, taking what they can for profit. Now the army wants to move in. The Indians are demanding protection of their lands, but their future is uncertain.

5

Plant Power

Some of the world's most amazing plants grow in the rain forest. There you'll see vines that grow as much as 3 feet a day, touch plants that have huge stomachs, and sniff flowers that smell like garbage. You'll feel palm fronds whose leaves are sharp enough to chop off a person's head, and discover trees that have more than a half million flowers. It's a bit different from the oak trees or cacti in your backyard!

The Pitcher Plant's Supper

To make your houseplants grow, would you feed them raw steak? Of course not! But some plants do eat meat. These plants are carnivores, just like jaguars, snakes, and wolves. (Don't worry, though. Meat-eating plants don't eat humans. That happens only in horror movies.) Carnivorous plants need more than sun, rain, and soil in order to survive. Since they're not equipped with sharp teeth or clutching claws, they must be much more subtle killers. To get extra nutrients, they trap and feed on insects and other small animals.

The *pitcher plant,* found in Southeast Asia, is built for killing. Its leaves cup together to form a large pitcher, which is filled with a deadly brew of digestive juices. Victims are lured to the pitcher plant by the strong scent of its nectar. While lapping up nectar along the plant's slippery edges, insects and other small animals fall into the pitcher and drown. The pitcher works like a stomach, using its poisonous juices to break food down into usable nutrients. Those juices turn even hard-shelled insects into a nourishing soup.

A pitcher plant starts out as a vine that climbs 60 feet up a tree. When it reaches the branches, it grows its pitcher. Pitchers can be as much as 12 inches long! They're always filled with dead insects and other small creatures. Sometimes even a frog or mouse gets caught inside. One animal that isn't eaten by the hungry plant, however, is the *crab spider.* It lives in the pitcher, just above the deadly brew. This spider doesn't need to work very hard for its food. It allows the pitcher plant to do the work of luring its prey! The spider simply casts a web across the upper part of the pitcher, then it waits. Some of the plant's victims fall into the web. When they do, they are dealt a deadly spider bite. The spider gets food and shelter from the pitcher plant, but no one knows what the plant gets in return!

Rotten Perfumes

Imagine that you're walking in the rain forest and you see an *orchid,* a magnificent tropical flower. Unable to resist, you rush to inhale its rich perfume only to discover that it smells like rotting meat. What a horror! The orchid may smell bad to you, but this is the key to its survival.

Obviously not all rain-forest flowers smell terrible. Orchids do have the most powerful perfumes, however. Some smell like fancy colognes, others smell like minty spices, and there's one that even smells like the medicine you use for chest colds. Yet what smells foul to you smells great to bats that feed on this flower. Bats are drawn to flowers that smell like rotting meat, old cheese, or musty attics. For this reason, bats play an important part in the way orchids reproduce.

Bats and other animals that fly help flowering plants reproduce through a process called *pollination.* Pollination takes place when pollen grains are transferred (carried by bats, birds, bees, and other insects) from the male part of the flower (the *stamen*) to the female part (the *pistil*). When this happens we say that the flower has been fertilized. *Fertilization* is the process that allows seeds to form, and from these seeds new plants eventually grow.

Different flowers attract different animals. Birds like flowers with brilliant colors, not dreamy perfumes. Although scents don't attract birds to flowers, they certainly work on flies, bats, and bees. The *rafflesia* flower, for example, is nicknamed "the corpse lily" because it smells like a dead body. Flies flock to the disgusting smell and end up pollinating the flower. A single rafflesia bloom measures 3 feet across and weighs 20 pounds! It's the world's largest flower.

Drugstore in the Trees

The *Gayo* Indians of Indonesia never need to visit a drugstore. Like everyone else, they do get sick. But instead of going to the drugstore for a prescription, they make their medicines from the plants they find in the forest. If they have a headache, for example, they simply eat some raw *Parkia* seeds. When these seeds are roasted and mashed, they cure a bad case of worms or heal a nasty cut quickly. The *Parkia* tree is just one of the 170 rain-forest plants that the Gayos and other tribal peoples have used for thousands of years to cure diseases. Through trial and error, they have learned which plants are helpful and which ones could harm them. They know, for example, that *strychnine* and *cyanide* are deadly poisons produced by the same rain-forest plants that have cured them of so many diseases.

In our society, too, more and more people are beginning to realize that the plants of the rain forest may contain the cures for some of today's most fatal diseases. Drugs that combat *malaria,* a disease carried by mosquitoes, and *leukemia,* a cancer of the blood that kills many people, come from rain-forest plants. A doctor observed how Indians used a poison called *curare* to make animals they hunted very sleepy so they'd be easier to catch! The doctor thought curare could be a good drug for making people sleepy before surgery. Today it is used in many operating rooms. One out of three medicines is made from tropical plants. Yet many cures may not be discovered because of the forest's uncertain future. As more and more of the rain forest is destroyed, so are its "miracle drug" plants. Among these plants could be the possible cure for many deadly diseases, including AIDS. That's why an international group of doctors and biologists began a program called Save the Plants That Save Lives. The group collects and grows tropical plants in an effort to save them from becoming extinct. They want to preserve the drugstore in the trees!

6

Going, Going, Gone?

By the time you reach the end of this sentence, a patch of rain forest as big as a football field will have been destroyed. By the end of the day, 48 species of plants and animals in the forest will also be gone forever. The mighty rain forest that has thrived for 200 million years may not be around by the time you're 65.

Furniture and Forest Fires

Human beings are destroying the rain forests. Around the world, people have tried to convert rain forests into land that can be used for farming and other purposes. The result has been deforestation. When an area is *deforested,* its trees are stripped away and the land is left bare. In Asia and Africa, loggers chop down huge sections of rain forest to find teak, mahogany, and walnut trees. Furniture manufacturers pay a great deal of money for these rare trees. Not only are the trees destroyed, but the homeland of many tribal peoples, such as the Penan and the Pygmies, are destroyed as well.

In Central and South America, rain forests are threatened by pioneers and cattle ranchers. When the Brazilian government offered free land in the rain forest, millions of poor people left the cities to accept the offer. Like the Yanomamis and other tribes, the pioneers practiced slash-and-burn farming to grow food. Millions of people burned plots in the forest, and many species of plants and animals were killed. Satellite images of Brazil show that enormous sections of the rain forest are little more than flaming infernos! Pioneers had set them on fire to clear the land for farming.

In addition to destroying the land, fires also cause air pollution. The heavy smoke turns the air into a thick, black cloud. Sometimes the smoke is so heavy that pilots are unable to fly overhead. The smoke also releases *carbon dioxide,* a gas that creates a kind of blanket in the Earth's atmosphere that traps the heat from the sun and prevents it from escaping into space as it should. This can lead to the *greenhouse effect*—the earth gets warmer and warmer because the atmosphere has been damaged.

Cattle ranchers also burn millions of acres to clear the land for grazing pastures. The United States is a big buyer of beef from the rain forest. This beef is used to make hamburgers, sandwich meats, pet food, and baby food. To produce a 4-ounce burger like the ones you buy from fast-food restaurants, an area of rain forest the size of a small kitchen is destroyed. Is that juicy little quarter-pounder worth such a high price? One of the largest fast-food restaurants in the United States is doing something to solve the problem. McDonald's refuses to buy rain-forest beef.

People pay a heavy price for making the rain forest "useful." Thousands of species of plants and animals found only in the rain forests are losing their *habitats*, or homes, and are becoming extinct. Medicines of the future are being destroyed before they have even been discovered. Heavy rains *erode*, or wash away, the deforested, naked soil. The once-fertile forest is turning into a desert where nothing can grow.

Hero of the Rain Forest

Chico Mendes realized the terrible plight of the rain forest many years ago. Mendes grew up in a rain forest in western Brazil. Like his father and grandfather, he was a rubber tapper. He tapped latex from wild rubber trees, then sold it to rubber manufacturers. (Rubber tapping doesn't kill a tree.) During the 1970's, Mendes and thousands of other tappers were ordered to move from their land by ranchers who wanted to turn it into pastures. Mendes refused to leave. He wanted to save both his job and the rain forest. He organized demonstrations to block the ranchers' bulldozers. On December 22, 1988, Chico Mendes was shot in the back by a rancher.

Iguana Burgers To Go

Since Mendes's death, the world has finally begun to realize that if we don't act quickly, the rain forest will vanish forever. If people can earn a living from the forest *without burning down trees,* there's a chance that it will survive. Biologist Dagmar Werner, known as the "Iguana Mama," hopes iguanas will guarantee the forest's future. *Iguanas* are animals that live in the canopy. They don't do well outside their natural habitat. Werner is teaching Panamanians how to raise iguanas to sell in the markets. One fat iguana can feed a large family. Iguana meat is an expensive treat throughout Latin America. However, it may take a while for iguana burgers to make it big in North America!

Other crops that grow in the rain forest are Brazil nuts and cashews. These plants won't survive on land that's been burned and cleared for farming. Every time you eat these nuts you're helping to keep the rain forest alive, because these crops are harvested from the *living* rain forest. Today small groups of South American farmers are trying to earn a living by growing cashews, Brazil nuts, and other rain-forest crops. The farmers sell the nuts around the world. Ben and Jerry's ice-cream company makes Rainforest Crunch ice cream using these nuts. Profits from the sales of this flavor are used to help teach more people how to farm the forest without destroying it.

What You Can Do

You can help save the rain forest by buying Brazil nuts—a product that can be harvested without burning the forest—and iguana burgers, if you happen to visit Central or South America. You can also boycott (refuse to buy) products that are made from tropical trees. Did you know that chopsticks are made from rain-forest trees? So is a lot of furniture.

As a class project, why not adopt an acre of rain forest? Contact The Nature Conservancy for information. Other groups you can write to for information are the Rainforest Alliance and the World Wildlife Fund. Act now to save the rain forest. Life on earth depends on it!

The Nature Conservancy
Adopt-an-Acre Program
1815 N. Lynn Street
Arlington, VA 22209

Rainforest Alliance
Suite 512
270 Lafayette Street
New York, NY 10012

World Wildlife Fund
1250 24th Street NW
Washington, D.C. 20037